Romeo and Juliet

by

William Shakespeare

Abridged by KJ O'Hara

Copyright © 2014 by KJ O'Hara

The right of KJ O'Hara to identify himself as adapter of this work is asserted by him under accordance of the Copyright, Designs and Patents Act, 1988

All rights reserved. Except as permitted under current legislation, no part of this work may be photocopied, stored in a retrieval system, published, performed in public, adapted, broadcast, transmitted, recorded or reproduced in any form by any means without prior permission of the copyright holder.
Permission for and licence to perform this version in public can be obtained from the address at the bottom of this page.

First Published 2014

Cover Illustration Copyright © Siloto

Although the adapter and publisher have made every effort to ensure that the information in this book was correct at press time, the adapter and publisher do not assume and hereby disclaim any liability to any party for any loss, damage, or disruption caused by errors or omissions, whether such errors or omissions result from negligence, accident, or any other cause.

ISBN: 978-1501052705
Published by Antic Mind
102 Dudwell Lane, Halifax, UK. HX30SH
All Enquiries to publisher@anticmind.com

Contents

Forward 5

Dramatis Personae 7

SCENE 1 8

SCENE 2 9

SCENE 3 12

SCENE 4 13

SCENE 5 15

SCENE 6 17

SCENE 7 19

SCENE 8 22

SCENE 9 24

SCENE 10 27

SCENE 11 29

SCENE 12 30

SCENE 13 33

SCENE 14 34

SCENE 15 36

SCENE 16 38

SCENE 17 40

SCENE 18 42

Forward

In abridging Romeo and Juliet for schools and performance I have brought together my experience as former Artistic Director of Antic Mind Theatre Company and of being an English and drama teacher for over 20 years. I originally abridged the play for a Theatre In Education production which successfully toured schools from 2002 to 2004 and was seen by thousands of students.

The aim was to produce a performance to be acted by a small cast playing multiple roles. I chose to shorten the length of performance to just over an hour because the audience was usually 11 to 16 year old students and having taught them Shakespeare for many years I knew that a pacy version, focusing on the essential elements of the play, would by keep them thoroughly enthralled. For that reason I have included what I consider to be everything an English teacher would want to see in an abridged version.

Although I have removed a few shorter scenes in their entirety, my main revisions have been to cut extraneous dialogue from all scenes. This was done partially to allow the play to be performed by a small cast and partially to make the play more exciting for a younger audience. As part of the abridgement, I have removed a small number of minor characters from the play.

As a drama teacher, I have used this version of the text many times with my students. Sometimes we have used it for exploration, at others it has been used as a script for performance. I have even used it as the basis to make even shorter abridgements for students to perform in small groups as examination pieces.

This version allows teachers the flexibility to perform the play with a large or small number of students. In the original Theatre In Education tour, restricted by what we could fit in a touring van and the costs of employing actors, we performed the play with just four actors.

KJ O'Hara

Dramatis Personae

Juliet	Capulet's daughter
Romeo	Montague's son
Mercutio	Kinsman to the Prince of Verona and friend of Romeo
Tybalt	Lady Capulet's nephew and Juliet's cousin
The Nurse	Juliet's nursemaid
Friar Laurence	A Franciscan brother
Capulet	Juliet's father
Paris	A noble kinsman to the Prince
Benvolio	Montague's nephew and Romeo's cousin
Lady Caputlet	Juliet's mother
Montague	Romeo's father
Balthasar	Romeo's servant
Apothacary	A chemist
Escalus	The Prince of Verona
Lady Montague	Romeo's mother
Abraham	A servant to Montague
Gregory	A servant to Capulet

SCENE 1
(Prologue)

CHORUS   Two households, both alike in dignity,
In fair Verona, where we lay our scene,
From ancient grudge break to new mutiny,
Where civil blood makes civil hands unclean.
From forth the fatal loins of these two foes
A pair of star-cross'd lovers take their life;
Whose misadventured piteous overthrows
Do with their death bury their parents' strife.
The fearful passage of their death-mark'd love,
And the continuance of their parents' rage,
Which, but their children's end, nought could remove,
Is now the two hours' traffic of our stage;
The which if you with patient ears attend,
What here shall miss, our toil shall strive to mend.

[Exit]

SCENE 2
(From Act I Scene1)

Verona. A public place

There is a public brawl between the Montegues and Capulets

GREGORY	Here comes one of the house of the Montagues. I will frown as I pass by, and let him take it as he list.
ABRAHAM	Do you bite your thumb at me, sir?
GREGORY	I do bite my thumb, sir.
ABRAHAM	Do you bite your thumb at me, sir?
GREGORY	No, sir, I do not bite my thumb at you, sir, But I bite my thumb, sir. Do you quarrel, sir?
ABRAHAM	Quarrel sir! no, sir.
GREGORY	If you do, sir, I am for you: I serve as good a man as you.
ABRAHAM	No better.
GREGORY	Well, sir.
ABRAHAM	Say 'better', here comes one of my master's kinsmen.
GREGORY	Yes, better, sir.
ABRAHAM	You lie.

[They begin to fight]

[Enter BENVOLIO]

BENVOLIO	Part, fools! Put up your swords; you know not what you do.

[Enter TYBALT]

TYBALT	What, art thou drawn among these heartless hinds? Turn thee, Benvolio, look upon thy death.

BENVOLIO   I do but keep the peace: put up thy sword,
                    Or manage it to part these men with me.

TYBALT   What, drawn, and talk of peace! I hate the word,
                    As I hate hell, all Montagues, and thee:
                    Have at thee, coward!

[Enter CAPULET]

CAPULET   What noise is this? Give me my long sword, ho!

[Enter MONTAGUE]

MONTAGUE   Thou villain Capulet.

[Enter PRINCE]

PRINCE   Rebellious subjects, enemies to peace,
                    On pain of torture, from those bloody hands
                    Throw your mistemper'd weapons to the ground.
                    Three civil brawls, bred of an airy word,
                    By thee, old Capulet, and Montague,
                    Have thrice disturb'd the quiet of our streets.
                    If ever you disturb our streets again,
                    Your lives shall pay the forfeit of the peace.
                    Once more, on pain of death, all men depart.

[Exeunt all except Benvolio. Enter Romeo]

ROMEO   Ay me! sad hours seem long.

BENVOLIO   What sadness lengthens Romeo's hours?

ROMEO   Not having that, which, having, makes them short.

BENVOLIO   In love?

ROMEO   Out!

BENVOLIO   Of love?

ROMEO   Out of her favour, where I am in love.

BENVOLIO   Tell me in sadness, who is that you love.

ROMEO   In sadness, cousin, I do love a woman.

BENVOLIO	I aim'd so near, when I supposed you loved.
ROMEO	A right good mark-man! And she's fair I love She'll not be hit with Cupid's arrow; she hath Dian's wit; And will not stay the siege of loving terms, Nor bide the encounter of assailing eyes, Nor ope her lap to saint-seducing gold: O, she is rich in beauty.
BENVOLIO	Then she hath sworn that she will still live chaste?
ROMEO	She hath, and in that sparing makes huge waste, She hath forsworn to love, and in that vow Do I live dead that live to tell it now.
BENVOLIO	Be ruled by me, forget to think of her.
ROMEO	O, teach me how I should forget to think.
BENVOLIO	By giving liberty unto thine eyes; Examine other beauties.
ROMEO	Farewell: thou canst not teach me to forget.
[Exeunt]	

SCENE 3
(From Act I Scene 2)

A Street

The County Paris asks Capulet if he can marry his daughter, Juliet

PARIS	But now, my lord, what say you to my suit?
CAPULET	But saying o'er what I have said before:
	My child is yet a stranger in the world;
	She hath not seen the change of fourteen years,
	Let two more summers wither in their pride,
	Ere we may think her ripe to be a bride.
	But woo her, gentle Paris, get her heart,
	My will to her consent is but a part;
	An she agree, within her scope of choice
	Lies my consent and fair according voice.
	This night I hold an old accustom'd feast,
	Whereto I have invited many a guest,
	Such as I love; and you, among the store,
	One more, most welcome, makes my number more.
	Come, go with me.

SCENE 4
(From Act I Scene 3)

A room in Capulet's house

Juliet's mother tries to find out whether Juliet would want to marry the County Paris

LADY CAPULET	Nurse, where's my daughter? call her forth to me.
NURSE	Now, by my maidenhead, at twelve year old, I bade her come. What, lamb! what, ladybird! God forbid! Where's this girl? What, Juliet!

[Enter JULIET]

JULIET	How now! who calls?
NURSE	Your mother.
JULIET	Madam, I am here. What is your will?
LADY CAPULET	This is the matter: nurse, give leave awhile, We must talk in secret: nurse, come back again; I have remember'd me, thou's hear our counsel. Thou know'st my daughter's of a pretty age.
NURSE	Faith, I can tell her age unto an hour.
LADY CAPULET	She's not fourteen.
NURSE	I'll lay fourteen of my teeth, And yet, to my teeth be it spoken, I have but four, She is not fourteen. How long is it now To Lammas-tide?
LADY CAPULET	A fortnight and odd days.
NURSE	Even or odd, of all days in the year, Come Lammas-eve at night shall she be fourteen. I remember it well. Of all the days of the year, upon that day: For I had then laid wormwood to my dug, When it did taste the wormwood on the nipple and felt it bitter, pretty fool,

	To see it tetchy and fall out with the dug!
	And since that time it is eleven years.
LADY CAPULET	Enough of this; I pray thee, hold thy peace.
NURSE	Peace, I have done. God mark thee to his grace!
	Thou wast the prettiest babe that e'er I nursed:
	An I might live to see thee married once,
	I have my wish.
LADY CAPULET	Marry, that 'marry' is the very theme
	I came to talk of. Tell me, daughter Juliet,
	How stands your disposition to be married?
JULIET	It is an honour that I dream not of.
NURSE	An honour! Were not I thine only nurse,
	I would say thou hadst suck'd wisdom from thy teat.
LADY CAPULET	Well, think of marriage now; younger than you,
	Here in Verona, ladies of esteem,
	Are made already mothers: by my count,
	I was your mother much upon these years
	That you are now a maid. Thus then in brief:
	The valiant Paris seeks you for his love.
NURSE	A man, young lady! lady, such a man
	As all the world. Why, he's a man of wax.
LADY CAPULET	Verona's summer hath not such a flower.
	What say you? can you love the gentleman?
JULIET	I'll look to like, if looking liking move:
	But no more deep will I endart mine eye
	Than your consent gives strength to make it fly.
NURSE	Go, girl, seek happy nights to happy days.
[Exeunt]	

SCENE 5
(From Act I Scene IV)

A street in Verona

Romeo, Benvolio and Mercutio meet before going to Capulet's feast

ROMEO	I am not for this ambling; we mean well in going to this mask; But 'tis no wit to go.
MERCUTIO	Why, may one ask?
ROMEO	I dream'd a dream to-night.
MERCUTIO	And so did I.
ROMEO	Well, what was yours?
MERCUTIO	That dreamers often lie.
ROMEO	In bed asleep, while they do dream things true.
MERCUTIO	O, then, I see Queen Mab hath been with you. She is the fairies' midwife, and she comes In shape no bigger than an agate-stone On the fore-finger of an alderman, Drawn with a team of little atomies Athwart men's noses as they lie asleep; Her wagon-spokes made of long spiders' legs, The cover of the wings of grasshoppers, The traces of the smallest spider's web, The collars of the moonshine's watery beams, Her whip of cricket's bone, the lash of film, Not so big as a round little worm Prick'd from the lazy finger of a maid; Her chariot is an empty hazel-nut Made by the joiner squirrel or old grub, Time out o' mind the fairies' coachmakers. And in this state she gallops night by night Through lovers' brains, and then they dream of love; O'er courtiers' knees, that dream on court'sies straight, O'er lawyers' fingers, who straight dream on fees, O'er ladies ' lips, who straight on kisses dream, Which oft the angry Mab with blisters plagues, Because their breaths with sweetmeats tainted are:

                Sometime she gallops o'er a courtier's nose,
                And then dreams he of smelling out a suit;
                And sometime comes she with a tithe-pig's tail
                Tickling a parson's nose as a' lies asleep,
                Then dreams, he of another benefice:
                This is that very Mab
                That plaits the manes of horses in the night,
                And bakes the elflocks in foul sluttish hairs,
                Which once untangled, much misfortune bodes:
                This is the hag, when maids lie on their backs,
                That presses them and learns them first to bear,
                Making them women of good carriage:
                This is she...

ROMEO   Peace, peace, Mercutio, peace!
                Thou talk'st of nothing.

MERCUTIO   True, I talk of dreams,
                Which are the children of an idle brain,
                Begot of nothing but vain fantasy,
                Which is as thin of substance as the air
                And more inconstant than the wind.

BENVOLIO   This wind, you talk of, blows us from ourselves;
                Supper is done, and we shall come too late.

ROMEO   I fear, too early: for my mind misgives
                Some consequence yet hanging in the stars
                Shall bitterly begin his fearful date
                With this night's revels.
                But He, that hath the steerage of my course,
                Direct my sail! On, lusty gentlemen.

[Exeunt]

SCENE 6
(From Act I Scene V)

A hall in Capulet's house

Romeo and Juliet meet at Capulet's feast

ROMEO	[Aside] What lady is that? O, she doth teach the torches to burn bright! It seems she hangs upon the cheek of night Like a rich jewel in an Ethiope's ear; Beauty too rich for use, for earth too dear! I'll watch her place of stand, And, touching hers, make blessed my rude hand. Did my heart love till now? forswear it, sight! For I ne'er saw true beauty till this night.
TYBALT	This, by his voice, should be a Montague. Now, by the stock and honour of my kin, To strike him dead, I hold it not a sin.
CAPULET	Why, how now, kinsman! wherefore storm you so?
TYBALT	Uncle, this is a Montague, our foe, A villain that is hither come in spite, To scorn at our solemnity this night.
CAPULET	Young Romeo is it? Let him alone; To say truth, Verona brags of him To be a virtuous and well-govern'd youth: I would not for the wealth of all the town Here in my house do him disparagement:
TYBALT	I'll not endure him.
CAPULET	He shall be endured: he shall: go to; Am I the master here, or you? You are a saucy boy: is't so, indeed? You are a princox; go:
TYBALT	I will withdraw: but this intrusion shall Now seeming sweet convert to bitter gall.
ROMEO	[To JULIET] If I profane with my unworthiest hand This holy shrine, the gentle fine is this:

	My lips, two blushing pilgrims, ready stand
	To smooth that rough touch with a tender kiss.
JULIET	Good pilgrim, you do wrong your hand too much,
	Which mannerly devotion shows in this;
	For saints have hands that pilgrims' hands do touch,
	And palm to palm is holy palmers' kiss.
ROMEO	Have not saints lips, and holy palmers too?
JULIET	Ay, pilgrim, lips that they must use in prayer.
ROMEO	O, then, dear saint, let lips do what hands do;
	They pray, grant thou, lest faith turn to despair.
JULIET	Saints do not move, though grant for prayers' sake.
ROMEO	Then move not, while my prayer's effect I take.
	Thus from my lips, by yours, my sin is purged.
JULIET	Then have my lips the sin that they have took.
ROMEO	Sin from thy lips? O trespass sweetly urged!
	Give me my sin again.
JULIET	You kiss by the book.
NURSE	Madam, your mother craves a word with you.
ROMEO	Is she a Capulet?
	O dear account! my life is my foe's debt.
JULIET	Come hither, nurse. What is yond gentleman?
NURSE	His name is Romeo, and a Montague;
	The only son of your great enemy.
JULIET	My only love sprung from my only hate!
	Too early seen unknown, and known too late!
	Prodigious birth of love it is to me,
	That I must love a loathed enemy.
[Exeunt]	

SCENE 7
(From Act II Scene II)

Capulet's orchard

Romeo sneaks into Capulet's orchard to try and see Juliet

[JULIET appears]

ROMEO
But, soft! what light through yonder window breaks?
It is the east, and Juliet is the sun.
Arise, fair sun, and kill the envious moon,
Who is already sick and pale with grief,
That thou her maid art far more fair than she:
It is my lady, O, it is my love!
O, that she knew she were!
See, how she leans her cheek upon her hand!
O, that I were a glove upon that hand,
That I might touch that cheek!

JULIET
Ay me!

ROMEO
She speaks:
O, speak again, bright angel! for thou art
As glorious to this night.

JULIET
O Romeo, Romeo! wherefore art thou Romeo?
Deny thy father and refuse thy name;
Or, if thou wilt not, be but sworn my love,
And I'll no longer be a Capulet.

ROMEO
[Aside] Shall I hear more, or shall I speak at this?

JULIET
Tis but thy name that is my enemy;
Thou art thyself, though not a Montague.
What's Montague? it is nor hand, nor foot,
Nor arm, nor face, nor any other part
Belonging to a man. O, be some other name!
What's in a name? that which we call a rose
By any other name would smell as sweet;
So Romeo would, were he not Romeo call'd,
Retain that dear perfection which he owes
Without that title. Romeo, doff thy name,
And for that name which is no part of thee
Take all myself.

ROMEO	I take thee at thy word:
	Call me but love, and I'll be new baptized;
	Henceforth I never will be Romeo.
JULIET	What man art thou that thus bescreen'd in night
	So stumblest on my counsel?
ROMEO	By a name I know not how to tell thee who I am:
	My name, dear saint, is hateful to myself,
	Because it is an enemy to thee;
	Had I it written, I would tear the word.
JULIET	My ears have not yet drunk a hundred words
	Of that tongue's utterance, yet I know the sound:
	Art thou not Romeo and a Montague?
ROMEO	Neither, fair saint, if either thee dislike.
JULIET	Dost thou love me? O gentle Romeo,
	If thou dost love, pronounce it faithfully.
ROMEO	Lady, by yonder blessed moon I swear
	That tips with silver all these fruit-tree tops...
JULIET	O, swear not by the moon, the inconstant moon,
	That monthly changes in her circled orb,
	Lest that thy love prove likewise variable.
ROMEO	What shall I swear by?
JULIET	Do not swear at all
	Or, if thou wilt, swear by thy gracious self,
	Which is the god of my idolatry,
	And I'll believe thee.
ROMEO	If my heart's dear love...
JULIET	Well, do not swear: although I joy in thee,
	I have no joy of this contract to-night:
	It is too rash, too unadvised, too sudden;
	Too like the lightning, which doth cease to be
	Ere one can say 'It lightens.' Sweet, good night!
	This bud of love, by summer's ripening breath,
	May prove a beauteous flower when next we meet.
	Good night, good night! as sweet repose and rest

>   Come to thy heart as that within my breast!

ROMEO   O, wilt thou leave me so unsatisfied?

JULIET   What satisfaction canst thou have to-night?

ROMEO   The exchange of thy love's faithful vow for mine.

JULIET   I gave thee mine before thou didst request it:
                   And yet I would it were to give again.

ROMEO   Wouldst thou withdraw it? for what purpose, love?

JULIET   But to be frank, and give it thee again.
                   If that thy bent of love be honourable,
                   Thy purpose marriage, send me word to-morrow,
                   By one that I'll procure to come to thee,
                   Where and what time thou wilt perform the rite;
                   And all my fortunes at thy foot I'll lay
                   And follow thee my lord throughout the world.
                   At what o'clock to-morrow
                   Shall I send to thee?

ROMEO   At the hour of nine.

JULIET   I will not fail: 'tis twenty years till then.

ROMEO   Sleep dwell upon thine eyes, peace in thy breast!
                   Would I were sleep and peace, so sweet to rest!
                   Hence will I to my ghostly father's cell,
                   His help to crave, and my dear hap to tell.

[Exeunt]

SCENE 8
(From Act II Scene III)

Friar Laurence's cell

Romeo goes to Friar Laurence to tell him about his intention to marry Juliet

ROMEO	Good morrow, father.
FR LAURENCE	What early tongue so sweet saluteth me? Young son, it argues a distemper'd head So soon to bid good morrow to thy bed: Therefore thy earliness doth me assure Thou art up-roused by some distemperature; Or if not so, then here I hit it right, Our Romeo hath not been in bed to-night.
ROMEO	That last is true; the sweeter rest was mine.
FR LAURENCE	God pardon sin! wast thou with Rosaline?
ROMEO	With Rosaline, my ghostly father? no; I have forgot that name, and that name's woe.
FR LAURENCE	That's my good son: but where hast thou been, then?
ROMEO	I have been feasting with mine enemy,
FR LAURENCE	Be plain, good son.
ROMEO	Then plainly know my heart's dear love is set On the fair daughter of rich Capulet: As mine on hers, so hers is set on mine; And all combined, save what thou must combine By holy marriage: but this I pray, That thou consent to marry us to-day.
FR LAURENCE	Holy Saint Francis, what a change is here! Is Rosaline, whom thou didst love so dear, So soon forsaken? young men's love then lies Not truly in their hearts, but in their eyes. Jesu Maria, what a deal of brine Hath wash'd thy sallow cheeks for Rosaline!

ROMEO Thou chid'st me oft for loving Rosaline.

FR LAURENCE For doting, not for loving, pupil mine.

ROMEO I pray thee, chide not; she whom I love now
Doth grace for grace and love for love allow;
The other did not so.

FR LAURENCE O, she knew well
Thy love did read by rote and could not spell.
But come, young waverer, come, go with me,
In one respect I'll thy assistant be;
For this alliance may so happy prove,
To turn your households' rancour to pure love.

ROMEO O, let us hence; I stand on sudden haste.

FR LAURENCE Wisely and slow; they stumble that run fast.

[Exeunt]

William Shakespeare

SCENE 9
(From Act II Scene IV)

A street

Romeo makes arrangements with the Nurse for his and Juliet's marriage

BENVOLIO	Tybalt, the kinsman of old Capulet, Hath sent a letter to Romeo's house.
MERCUTIO	A challenge, on my life.
BENVOLIO	Romeo will answer it.
MERCUTIO	Any man that can write may answer a letter.
BENVOLIO	Nay, he will answer the letter's master, how he dares, being dared.
MERCUTIO	Alas poor Romeo! he is already dead; stabbed with a white wench's black eye; shot through the ear with a love-song; the very pin of his heart cleft with the blind bow-boy's butt-shaft: and is he a man to encounter Tybalt?
BENVOLIO	Why, what is Tybalt?
MERCUTIO	More than prince of cats, I can tell you. O, he is the courageous captain of compliments. He fights as you sing prick-song, keeps time, distance, and proportion; rests me his minim rest, one, two, and the third in your bosom: the very butcher of a silk button, a duellist, a duellist; a gentleman of the very first house, of the first and second cause: ah, the immortal passado! the punto reverso! The hai!
BENVOLIO	The what?
MERCUTIO	The pox of such antic, lisping, affecting Fantasticoes; these new tuners of accents! 'By Jesu, A very good blade! a very tall man! a very good whore!'
[Enter ROMEO]	
BENVOLIO	Here comes Romeo.

MERCUTIO	Signior Romeo, bon jour! You gave us the counterfeit fairly last night.
ROMEO	Good morrow to you both. What counterfeit did I give you?
MERCUTIO	The slip, sir, the slip; can you not conceive?
ROMEO	Pardon, good Mercutio, my business was great; and in Such a case as mine a man may strain courtesy. Here's goodly gear!

[Enter Nurse]

MERCUTIO	A sail, a sail!
NURSE	My fan.
MERCUTIO	To hide her face; for her fan's the fairer face.
NURSE	God ye good morrow, gentlemen.
MERCUTIO	God ye good den, fair gentlewoman.
NURSE	Is it good den?
MERCUTIO	'Tis no less, I tell you, for the bawdy hand of the dial is now upon the prick of noon.
NURSE	Out upon you! what a man are you! Gentlemen, can any of you tell me Where I may find the young Romeo?
ROMEO	I can tell you; but young Romeo will be older when You have found him than he was when you sought him: I am the youngest of that name, for fault of a worse.
NURSE	If you be he, sir, I desire some confidence with you.
ROMEO	I will follow you.
MERCUTIO	Farewell, ancient lady; farewell,

[Exeunt MERCUTIO and BENVOLIO]

NURSE	Pray you, sir, a word: my young lady bade

          me inquire you out; what she bade me say,
          I will keep to myself: but first let me tell ye,
          if ye should lead her into a fool's paradise, as they say,
          it were a very gross kind of behaviour,
          As they say: for the gentlewoman is young;
          And, therefore, if you should deal double with her,
          Truly it were an ill thing to be offered
          To any gentlewoman, and very weak dealing.

ROMEO   Nurse, commend me to thy lady and mistress.
                    I protest unto thee.

NURSE   Good heart, and, i' faith, I will tell her as much:
                    Lord, Lord, she will be a joyful woman.

ROMEO   Bid her devise some means to come to shrift this afternoon;
                    And there she shall at Friar Laurence' cell
                    Be shrived and married.

NURSE   This afternoon, sir? well, she shall be there.

ROMEO   Farewell; be trusty, and I'll quit thy pains:
                    Farewell; commend me to thy mistress.

NURSE   Ay, a thousand times.

[Exit]

SCENE 10
(From Act II Scene V)

Capulet's orchard

Juliet awaits the return of the Nurse and news from Romeo

JULIET	The clock struck nine when I did send the nurse;
	In half an hour she promised to return.
	From nine till twelve
	Is three long hours, yet she is not come.
	Had she affections and warm youthful blood,
	She would be as swift in motion as a ball;
	O God, she comes!
	O honey nurse, what news? Hast thou met with him?.
	How, good sweet nurse. O Lord, why look'st thou sad?
	Though news be sad, yet tell them merrily.
NURSE	I am a-weary, give me leave awhile:
	Fie, how my bones ache! what a jaunt have I had!
JULIET	I would thou hadst my bones, and I thy news:
	Nay, come, I pray thee, speak; good, good nurse, speak.
NURSE	Jesu, what haste? can you not stay awhile?
	Do you not see that I am out of breath?
JULIET	How art thou out of breath, when thou hast breath
	To say to me that thou art out of breath?
	Is thy news good, or bad?
	Let me be satisfied, is't good or bad?
Nurse	Well, you have made a simple choice; you know not
	How to choose a man: Romeo! no, not he; though his
	Face be better than any man's, yet his leg excels
	All men's; and for a hand, and a foot, and a body,
	Though they be not to be talked on, yet they are
	Past compare: he is not the flower of courtesy,
	But, I'll warrant him, as gentle as a lamb. Go thy
	Ways, wench; serve God. What, have you dined at home?
JULIET	No, no: but all this did I know before.
	What says he of our marriage? what of that?
Nurse	Lord, how my head aches! what a head have I!

	It beats as it would fall in twenty pieces.
	My back o' t' other side. O, my back, my back!
	Beshrew your heart for sending me about,
	To catch my death with jaunting up and down!

JULIET I' faith, I am sorry that thou art not well.
Sweet, sweet, sweet nurse, tell me, what says my love?

Nurse Your love says, like an honest gentleman, and a
courteous, and a kind, and a handsome, and, I
warrant, a virtuous... Where is your mother?

JULIET Where is my mother! why, she is within;
Where should she be? How oddly thou repliest!
'Your love says, like an honest gentleman,
Where is your mother?'

Nurse O God's lady dear!
Are you so hot? marry, come up, I trow;
Is this the poultice for my aching bones?
Henceforward do your messages yourself.

JULIET Here's such a coil! come, what says Romeo?

Nurse Have you got leave to go to shrift to-day?

JULIET I have.

Nurse Then hie you hence to Friar Laurence' cell;
There stays a husband to make you a wife:
Now comes the wanton blood up in your cheeks,
They'll be in scarlet straight at any news.
Hie you to church; I must another way,
To fetch a ladder, by the which your love
Must climb a bird's nest soon when it is dark:
I am the drudge and toil in your delight,
But you shall bear the burden soon at night.
Go; I'll to dinner: hie you to the cell.

JULIET Hie to high fortune! Honest nurse, farewell.

[Exeunt]

SCENE 11
(From Act II Scene VI)

Friar Laurence's cell

Romeo and Juliet get married

FR LAURENCE So smile the heavens upon this holy act,
That after hours with sorrow chide us not!

ROMEO Amen, amen! but come what sorrow can,
It cannot countervail the exchange of joy
That one short minute gives me in her sight.

FR LAURENCE These violent delights have violent ends
And in their triumph die, like fire and powder,
Therefore love moderately; long love doth so;
Too swift arrives as tardy as too slow.

[Enter JULIET]

Here comes the lady:

JULIET Good even to my ghostly confessor.

FR LAURENCE Come, come with me, and we will make short work;
For, by your leaves, you shall not stay alone
Till holy church incorporate two in one.

[Exeunt]

William Shakespeare

SCENE 12
(From Act III Scene 1)

A public place

Tybalt comes looking for vengeance on Romeo

BENVOLIO	The day is hot, the Capulets abroad, And, if we meet, we shall not scape a brawl; For now, these hot days, is the mad blood stirring. By my head, here come the Capulets.
MERCUTIO	By my heel, I care not.

[Enter TYBALT]

TYBALT	Mercutio, thou consort'st with Romeo.
MERCUTIO	Consort! what, dost thou make us minstrels? an thou make minstrels of us, look to hear nothing but discords: here's my fiddlestick; here's that shall make you dance. 'Zounds, consort!

[Enter ROMEO]

TYBALT	Well, peace be with you, sir: here comes my man.
MERCUTIO	But I'll be hanged, sir, if he wear your livery.
TYBALT	Romeo, the hate I bear thee can afford No better term than this: thou art a villain.
ROMEO	Tybalt, the reason that I have to love thee Doth much excuse the appertaining rage To such a greeting: villain am I none; Therefore farewell; I see thou know'st me not.
TYBALT	Boy, this shall not excuse the injuries That thou hast done me; therefore turn and draw.
ROMEO	I do protest, I never injured thee, But love thee better than thou canst devise, Till thou shalt know the reason of my love: And so, good Capulet, which name I tender As dearly as my own, be satisfied.

MERCUTIO	O calm, dishonourable, vile submission! Tybalt, you rat-catcher, will you walk?
TYBALT	What wouldst thou have with me?
MERCUTIO	Good king of cats, nothing but one of your nine lives; that I mean to make bold withal, and as you shall use me hereafter, drybeat the rest of the eight.
TYBALT	I am for you. [Drawing his sword.]
ROMEO	Gentle Mercutio, put thy rapier up.
MERCUTIO	Come, sir, your passado. [They fight]
ROMEO	Gentlemen, for shame, forbear this outrage! Tybalt, Mercutio, the prince expressly hath Forbidden bandying in Verona streets: Hold, Tybalt! good Mercutio!

[TYBALT stabs MERCUTIO under ROMEO's arm and flies]

MERCUTIO	I am hurt. A plague o' both your houses! I am sped.
BENVOLIO	What, art thou hurt?
MERCUTIO	Ay, ay, a scratch, a scratch; marry, 'tis enough.
ROMEO	Courage, man; the hurt cannot be much.
MERCUTIO	No, 'tis not so deep as a well, nor so wide as a church-door; but 'tis enough, 'twill serve: ask for me to-morrow, and you shall find me a grave man. A plague o' both your houses! Why the devil came you between us? I was hurt under your arm.
ROMEO	I thought all for the best.
MERCUTIO	A plague o' both your houses! They have made worms' meat of me: I have it, And soundly too: your houses!

[Enter Tybalt]

ROMEO   Alive, in triumph! and Mercutio slain!
        Now, Tybalt, take the villain back again,
        That late thou gavest me; for Mercutio's soul
        Is but a little way above our heads,
        Staying for thine to keep him company:
        Either thou, or I, or both, must go with him.

TYBALT Thou, wretched boy, that didst consort him here,
        Shalt with him hence.

ROMEO   This shall determine that.

[They fight; TYBALT is slain]

ROMEO   O, I am fortune's fool!

[Exit ROMEO then Enter PRINCE]

PRINCE Benvolio, who began this bloody fray?

BENVOLIO Tybalt, here slain, whom Romeo's hand did slay;
        Romeo that spoke him fair and urged withal
        Your high displeasure: all this uttered with gentle breath,
        Could not take truce with the unruly spleen
        Of Tybalt deaf to peace, but that he tilts
        With piercing steel at bold Mercutio's breast.
        Romeo he cries aloud, 'Hold, friends! friends, part!'
        And 'twixt them rushes; underneath whose arm
        An envious thrust from Tybalt hit the life
        Of stout Mercutio, and then Tybalt fled;
        But by and by comes back to Romeo,
        Who had but newly entertain'd revenge,
        And ere I could draw to part them, was stout Tybalt slain.

PRINCE Romeo slew him, he slew Mercutio;
        Who now the price of his dear blood doth owe?
        Romeo was Mercutio's friend;
        His fault concludes but what the law should end,
        The life of Tybalt. And for that offence
        Immediately we do exile him hence:
        Therefore let Romeo hence in haste,
        Else, when he's found, that hour is his last.

[Exeunt]

SCENE 13
(From Act III Scene II)

Capulet's orchard

Juliet finds out Romeo has killed her cousin and has been banished

JULIET	Come, night; come, Romeo; come, thou day in night;
	For thou wilt lie upon the wings of night
	Whiter than new snow on a raven's back.
	Come, gentle night, come, loving, black-brow'd night,
	Give me my Romeo.

[Enter NURSE]

NURSE	Ah, well-a-day! he's dead, he's dead, he's dead!
	We are undone, lady, we are undone!
	Alack the day! he's gone, he's kill'd, he's dead!

JULIET	What storm is this that blows so contrary?

NURSE	Tybalt is gone, and Romeo banished;
	Romeo that kill'd him, he is banished.

JULIET	O God! did Romeo's hand shed Tybalt's blood?
	'Tybalt is dead, and Romeo banished;'
	That 'banished,' that one word 'banished,'
	Hath slain ten thousand Tybalts. Tybalt's death
	Was woe enough, if it had ended there:
	'Romeo is banished!'
	There is no end, no limit, measure, bound,
	In that word's death; no words can that woe sound.

NURSE	Hie to your chamber: I'll find Romeo
	To comfort you: I wot well where he is.
	Hark ye, your Romeo will be here at night:
	I'll to him; he is hid at Laurence' cell.

JULIET	O, find him! give this ring to my true knight,
	And bid him come to take his last farewell.

[Exeunt]

William Shakespeare

SCENE 14
(From Act III Scene V)

Juliet's Bedchamber

Romeo and Juliet wake to the realisation that he has to leave Verona

JULIET
Wilt thou be gone? it is not yet near day:
It was the nightingale, and not the lark,
That pierced the fearful hollow of thine ear;
Nightly she sings on yon pomegranate-tree:
Believe me, love, it was the nightingale.

ROMEO
It was the lark, the herald of the morn,
No nightingale: look, love, what envious streaks
Do lace the severing clouds in yonder east:
Night's candles are burnt out, and jocund day
Stands tiptoe on the misty mountain tops.
I must be gone and live, or stay and die.

JULIET
Yon light is not day-light, I know it, I:
It is some meteor that the sun exhales,
To be to thee this night a torch-bearer,
And light thee on thy way to Mantua:
Therefore stay yet; thou need'st not to be gone.

ROMEO
Let me be ta'en, let me be put to death;
I am content, so thou wilt have it so.
I have more care to stay than will to go:
Come, death, and welcome! Juliet wills it so.
How is't, my soul? let's talk; it is not day.

JULIET
It is, it is: hie hence, be gone, away!
It is the lark that sings so out of tune,
Straining harsh discords and unpleasing sharps.
O, now be gone; more light and light it grows.

ROMEO
Farewell, farewell!

JULIET
O think'st thou we shall ever meet again?

ROMEO
I doubt it not; and all these woes shall serve
For sweet discourses in our time to come.

[Exit Romeo, Enter CAPULET and Lady CAPULET]

LADY CAPULET   Why, how now, Juliet!
Evermore weeping for your cousin's death?
What, wilt thou wash him from his grave with tears?
But now I'll tell thee joyful tidings, girl.

JULIET   And joy comes well in such a needy time:
What are they, I beseech your ladyship?

LADY CAPULET   Marry, my child, early next Thursday morn,
The gallant, young and noble gentleman,
The County Paris, at Saint Peter's Church,
Shall happily make thee there a joyful bride.

JULIET   Now, by Saint Peter's Church and Peter too,
He shall not make me there a joyful bride.
I pray you, my lord and father,
I will not marry yet; and, when I do, I swear,
It shall be Romeo, whom you know I hate,
Rather than Paris. These are news indeed!

CAPULET   How now, how now, chop-logic! What is this?
'Proud,' and 'I thank you,' and 'I thank you not;'
And yet 'not proud,' mistress minion, you,
Thank me no thankings, nor, proud me no prouds,
But fettle your fine joints 'gainst Thursday next,
To go with Paris to Saint Peter's Church,
Or I will drag thee on a hurdle thither.

JULIET   Good father, I beseech you on my knees,

CAPULET   Hang thee, young baggage! disobedient wretch!
I tell thee what: get thee to church o' Thursday,
Or never after look me in the face:
Speak not, reply not, do not answer me;
My fingers itch. Look to't, think on't.
Thursday is near; lay hand on heart, advise:
An you be mine, I'll give you to my friend;
And you be not, hang, beg, starve, die in the streets,
For, by my soul, I'll ne'er acknowledge thee,
Nor what is mine shall never do thee good.

[Exeunt]

SCENE 15
(From Act IV Scene 1)

Friar Laurence's cell

Juliet meets with Friar Laurence in the hope of finding a way not to marry Paris

JULIET	O shut the door! and when thou hast done so,
	Come weep with me; past hope, past cure, past help!
FR LAURENCE	Ah, Juliet, I already know thy grief;
	It strains me past the compass of my wits:
	I hear thou must, on Thursday next be married to this county.
JULIET	Tell me not, friar, that thou hear'st of this,
	Unless thou tell me how I may prevent it:
	If, in thy wisdom, thou canst give no help,
	Do thou but call my resolution wise,
	And with this knife I'll help it presently.
	Be not so long to speak; I long to die,
	If what thou speak'st speak not of remedy.
FR LAURENCE	Hold, daughter: I do spy a kind of hope,
	If, rather than to marry County Paris,
	Thou hast the strength of will to slay thyself,
	Then is it likely thou wilt undertake
	A thing like death to chide away this shame,
	And, if thou darest, I'll give thee remedy.
JULIET	O, shut me nightly in a charnel-house,
	O'er-cover'd quite with dead men's rattling bones,
	With reeky shanks and yellow chapless skulls;
	And I will do it without fear or doubt,
	To live an unstain'd wife to my sweet love.
FR LAURENCE	Hold, then; go home, be merry, give consent
	To marry Paris: To-morrow night
	Take thou this vial, being then in bed,
	And this distilled liquor drink thou off;
	When presently through all thy veins shall run
	A cold and drowsy humour, for no pulse
	Shall keep his native progress, but surcease:
	No warmth, no breath, shall testify thou livest;
	Each part, deprived of supple government,

	Shall, stiff and stark and cold, appear like death:
	And in this borrow'd likeness of shrunk death
	Thou shalt continue two and forty hours,
	And then awake as from a pleasant sleep.
	Now, when the bridegroom in the morning comes
	To rouse thee from thy bed, there art thou dead:
	Then, as the manner of our country is,
	Thou shalt be borne to that same ancient vault
	Where all the kindred of the Capulets lie.
	In the meantime, against thou shalt awake,
	Shall Romeo by my letters know our drift,
	And hither shall he come: and he and I
	Will watch thy waking, and that very night
	Shall Romeo bear thee hence to Mantua.
JULIET	Give me, give me! O, tell not me of fear!
FR LAURENCE	Hold; get you gone, be strong and prosperous
	In this resolve: I'll send a friar with speed
	To Mantua, with my letters to thy lord.
JULIET	Love give me strength! Farewell, dear father!

[Exeunt]

SCENE 16
(From Act IV Scenes III to V)

Hall in Capulet's house

Juliet carries out the plan she has made with Friar Laurence

CAPULET	How now, my headstrong! where have you been gadding?

JULIET	Where I have learn'd me to repent the sin
Of disobedient opposition
and am enjoin'd by holy Laurence to beg your pardon.
Henceforward I am ever ruled by you.

CAPULET	Send for the county; go tell him of this:
I'll have this knot knit up to-morrow morning.

[Exit Capulet]

JULIET	Farewell! God knows when we shall meet again.
Come, vial. What if this mixture do not work at all?
Shall I be married then to-morrow morning?
No, no: this shall forbid it: lie thou there.
What if it be a poison, which the friar
Subtly hath minister'd to have me dead,
Lest in this marriage he should be dishonour'd,
Because he married me before to Romeo?
Or, if I live, is it not very like,
if I wake, shall I not be distraught,
Environed with all these hideous fears?
And madly play with my forefather's joints?
And pluck the mangled Tybalt from his shroud?
And, in this rage, with some great kinsman's bone,
As with a club, dash out my desperate brains?
Romeo, I come! this do I drink to thee.

[Enter Nurse]

NURSE	Mistress! what, mistress! Juliet! fast, I warrant her,
Why, lamb! why, lady! fie, you slug-a-bed!
Marry, and amen, how sound is she asleep!
I must needs wake her. Madam, madam, madam!
Ay, let the county take you in your bed;
He'll fright you up, i' faith. Will it not be?
Lady! lady! lady! Alas, alas! Help, help! my lady's dead!

              O, well-a-day, that ever I was born!
              Some aqua vitae, ho! My lord!

CAPULET   Despised, distressed, hated, martyr'd, kill'd!
              Uncomfortable time, why camest thou now
              To murder, murder our solemnity?
              O child! O child! my soul, and not my child!
              Dead art thou! Alack! my child is dead;
              And with my child my joys are buried.

[Exeunt]

SCENE 17
(From Act V Scene I)

Mantua. A street

Romeo hears news that Juliet has died

ROMEO	How now, Balthasar! How doth my lady? How fares my Juliet? that I ask again; For nothing can be ill, if she be well.
BALTHASAR	Then she is well, and nothing can be ill: Her body sleeps in Capel's monument, And her immortal part with angels lives. I saw her laid low in her kindred's vault, And presently took post to tell it you.
ROMEO	Is it even so? then I defy you, stars! Thou know'st my lodging: get me ink and paper, And hire post-horses; I will hence to-night.
BALTHASAR	I do beseech you, sir, have patience: Your looks are pale and wild, and do import Some misadventure.
ROMEO	Leave me, and do the thing I bid thee do. Hast thou no letters to me from the friar?
BALTHASAR	No, my good lord.
ROMEO	No matter: get thee gone, And hire those horses; I'll be with thee straight.

[Exit BALTHASAR]

    Well, Juliet, I will lie with thee to-night.
    Let's see for means: O mischief, thou art swift
    To enter in the thoughts of desperate men!
    I do remember an apothecary,
    And hereabouts he dwells,
    And in his needy shop to myself I said
    'An if a man did need a poison now,
    Whose sale is present death in Mantua,
    Here lives a caitiff wretch would sell it him.'
    O, this same thought did but forerun my need;

And this same needy man must sell it me.

[Enter APOTHECARY]

APOTHECARY Who calls so loud?

ROMEO Come hither, man. I see that thou art poor:
Hold, there is forty ducats: let me have
A dram of poison, such soon-speeding gear
As will disperse itself through all the veins
That the life-weary taker may fall dead
As violently as hasty powder fired
Doth hurry from the fatal cannon's womb.

APOTHECARY Such mortal drugs I have; but Mantua's law
Is death to any he that utters them.

ROMEO Art thou so bare and full of wretchedness,
And fear'st to die? Famine is in thy cheeks,
Need and oppression starveth in thine eyes,
Contempt and beggary hangs upon thy back;
The world is not thy friend nor the world's law;
The world affords no law to make thee rich;
Then be not poor, but break it, and take this.

APOTHECARY My poverty, but not my will, consents.

ROMEO I pay thy poverty, and not thy will.

APOTHECARY Put this in any liquid thing you will,
And drink it off; and, if you had the strength
Of twenty men, it would dispatch you straight.

ROMEO Farewell: buy food, and get thyself in flesh.
Come, cordial and not poison, go with me
To Juliet's grave; for there must I use thee.

[Exeunt]

SCENE 18
(From Act V Scene III)

A churchyard; in it a tomb belonging to the Capulets

Romeo returns to Verona to see Juliet's body and end his life

PARIS
: Sweet flower, with flowers thy bridal bed I strew,
O woe! thy canopy is dust and stones;
Which with sweet water nightly I will dew,
Or, wanting that, with tears distill'd by moans:
The obsequies that I for thee will keep
Nightly shall be to strew thy grave and weep.

[Enter ROMEO]

PARIS
: This is that banish'd haughty Montague,
That murder'd my love's cousin, with which grief,
It is supposed, the fair creature died;
And here is come to do some villainous shame
To the dead bodies: I will apprehend him.
Stop thy unhallow'd toil, vile Montague!
Can vengeance be pursued further than death?
Condemned villain, I do apprehend thee:
Obey, and go with me; for thou must die.

ROMEO
: I must indeed; and therefore came I hither.
Good gentle youth, tempt not a desperate man;
Fly hence, and leave me: I beseech thee, youth,
Put not another sin upon my head,
By urging me to fury: O, be gone!

PARIS
: I do defy thy conjurations,
And apprehend thee for a felon here.

ROMEO
: Wilt thou provoke me? then have at thee, boy!

[They fight]

PARIS
: O, I am slain!

ROMEO
: Ah, dear Juliet,
Why art thou yet so fair? I still will stay with thee;
And never from this palace of dim night
Depart again: here, here will I remain

With worms that are thy chamber-maids; O, here
Will I set up my everlasting rest,
From this world-wearied flesh. Eyes, look your last!
Arms, take your last embrace! and, lips, O you
The doors of breath, seal with a righteous kiss
A dateless bargain to engrossing death!
Come, bitter conduct, come, unsavoury guide!
Here's to my love!

[Drinks]

O true apothecary!
Thy drugs are quick. Thus with a kiss I die.

[ROMEO dies then JULIET wakes]

JULIET Where is my lord? I do remember well where I should be,
And there I am. Where is my Romeo?
What's here? a cup, closed in my true love's hand?
Poison, I see, hath been his timeless end:
O churl! drunk all, and left no friendly drop
To help me after? I will kiss thy lips;
Haply some poison yet doth hang on them,
To make die with a restorative.
Thy lips are warm. Then I'll be brief.
O happy dagger! This is thy sheath;
there rust, and let me die.

[Falls on ROMEO's body, and dies]

[Enter PRINCE, CAPULET and MONTEGUE]

PRINCE Where be these enemies? Capulet! Montague!
See, what a scourge is laid upon your hate,
That heaven finds means to kill your joys with love.
And I for winking at your discords too
Have lost a brace of kinsmen: all are punish'd.

CAPULET O brother Montague, give me thy hand:
This is my daughter's jointure, for no more
Can I demand.

MONTAGUE But I can give thee more:
I will raise her statue in pure gold;
That while Verona by that name is known,
There shall no figure at such rate be set
As that of true and faithful Juliet.

CAPULET

        As rich shall Romeo's by his lady's lie;
        Poor sacrifices of our enmity!

PRINCE

        A glooming peace this morning with it brings;
        The sun, for sorrow, will not show his head:
        Go hence, to have more talk of these sad things;
        Some shall be pardon'd, and some punished:
        For never was a story of more woe
        Than this of Juliet and her Romeo.

[Exeunt]

ALSO AVAILABLE IN THIS SERIES

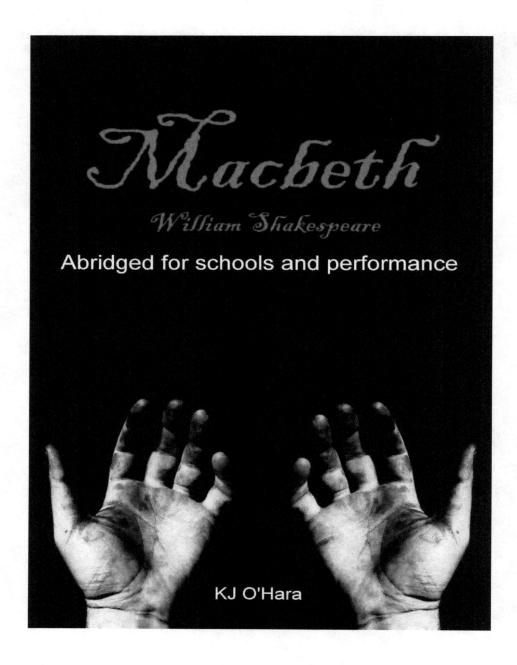

CPSIA information can be obtained
at www.ICGtesting.com
Printed in the USA
BVHW020147130523
664117BV00009B/181